KT-140-621

002135

A
TECHNICAL HISTORY
OF COSTUME

*

ANCIENT EGYPTIAN, ASSYRIAN, AND PERSIAN COSTUMES

In Preparation

ANCIENT GREEK, ROMAN AND BYZANTINE COSTUME AND DECORATIONS.

EUROPEAN COSTUME FROM THE THIRTEENTH CENTURY TO THE COMMENCEMENT OF THE SEVENTEENTH CENTURY—WITH DECORATIONS.

TYPES OF INDIAN, PERSIAN, CHINESE AND JAPANESE COSTUME AND DECORATIONS. With Notes on Various Additional Types of Primitive Garments. . . .

AGENTS

AMERICA . . . . THE MACMILLAN COMPANY
64 & 66 Fifth Avenue, NEW YORK

AUSTRALASIA . . . OXFORD UNIVERSITY PRESS
205 Flinders Lane, MELBOURNE

CANADA . . . . . . THE MACMILLAN COMPANY OF CANADA, LTD.
St. Martin's House, 70 Bond Street, TORONTO

INDIA . . . . MACMILLAN & COMPANY, LTD.
Macmillan Building, BOMBAY
309 Bow Bazaar Street, CALCUTTA

ANCIENT EGYPTIAN ASSYRIAN AND PERSIAN COSTUMES

AND DECORATIONS

BY

MARY G. HOUSTON

AND

FLORENCE S. HORNBLOWER

CONTAINING TWENTY-FIVE FULL-PAGE ILLUSTRATIONS, SIXTEEN OF THEM IN COLOUR, AND SIXTY LINE DIAGRAMS IN THE TEXT

A. & C. BLACK, LIMITED
4, 5 & 6 SOHO SQUARE, LONDON, W. 1.
1920

INTRODUCTION

If this work is to be kept within its limitations, it is naturally impossible to give a complete survey of all the varieties of the various styles. To get this knowledge it will be necessary to consult the works of reference, of which lists are given in each section. On the other hand, the special aspect of the work is more fully treated than in any other accessible book upon the subject.

Every illustration of costume given has been actually cut out and made up before being sketched, except in a few cases which are of the nature of duplicates, so that by following the directions given it will be easy for anyone to reproduce them in material. Where decoration is required, the exact drawing and colouring of the various styles of Historic Ornament, which are the work of F. S. Hornblower (who has also coloured the costumes where necessary), will enable such details to be appropriately applied.

Throughout the book, the illustrations are given by means of facsimiles of drawings by artists of the various centuries, so that a historic survey of the History of Figure Drawing will be included. Where the drawings of primitive artists do not clearly express the ideas intended to be conveyed, a modern drawing of the garment on a dress-stand will be used for explanation of the measured drawings of the cut-out garments. The growing appreciation of the beauty and value of the earlier and more primitive systems of cutting shown in modern dress designing for the last decade, when the so-called Magyar blouse (really the simple tunic common to all primitive folk) began to be popular, will make the present volume a convenient form of inspiration for designers; also, where more exact reproduction is needed, as in theatrical work, pageantry, and so forth, the careful working out of the details of cut and decoration will expedite production and save hours of fruitless searching in reference libraries.

To the Art Student, in addition to the always interesting history of costume, the development of the Art of Representation, as shown in the illustrations of these volumes, which is so strangely repeated in the personal history of every young person learning to draw, will be attractive and instructive. Finally, in connection with the history lesson in the ordinary school, teachers will find the illustrations clear and helpful, especially if dramatic representations are attempted.

MARY G. HOUSTON.

CONTENTS

LIST OF PLATES

IN COLOUR

LIST OF ILLUSTRATIONS

IN THE TEXT, OTHER THAN PLANS

LIST OF CUT OUT PATTERNS OR PLANS OF GARMENTS

LIST OF DATED GARMENTS

ILLUSTRATED

ANCIENT EGYPTIAN SECTION

ANCIENT ASSYRIAN SECTION

ANCIENT PERSIAN SECTION

DECORATION

ANCIENT EGYPTIAN COSTUME

GENERAL DESCRIPTION
OF
ANCIENT EGYPTIAN COSTUME

CUTTING OUT

As far as the cutting out of ancient Egyptian costume is concerned, we may divide it broadly into four types—namely: (1) The type of the *tunic*. (2) The type of the *robe*. (3) The type of the *skirt*, with or without cape. (4) The type of the *shawl* or *drapery*. The one or two varieties which occur in addition to these may be found in military dress and adaptations from the costumes of other countries. All the varieties above referred to are described in detail in this volume.

DECORATION AND COLOURING

Though we find Egyptian costume in many instances decorated all over with woven or printed patterns, decoration in the main was confined to accessories such as the head-dress, collar, and girdle, these being often painted, embroidered, beaded, or jewelled. See various examples given. The colouring which was usually, though not invariably, confined to the decorations consisted of simple schemes, variations of the hues of red, blue, green, yellow, and deep purple described on p. 66.

MATERIAL

The material used in the costumes was chiefly linen. In the most ancient types it was of a fairly thick, coarse weave; but in the later examples a fine thin linen, loosely woven so as to appear almost transparent, was used. The linen has often a stiffened appearance, and also gives the idea of having been goffered or pleated.

DATES

The earliest types of costume were the tunics; midway come the robes and skirts, and the draped or shawl type of costume appears the latest. However, the older types of costume did not disappear as the new ones were introduced, but all continued to be worn contemporaneously. The dates of most of the costumes in this volume are given with their description, and have been verified at the British Museum.

MEN AND WOMEN: THE DIFFERENCE IN THEIR DRESS

It can easily be gathered from the illustrations that the types of costume worn by both sexes were very similar. The high waist-line prevails in feminine dress, while the male costume, if girded, was generally confined about the hips.

Egyptian Works oj Reference.

Prisse d'Avennes, "L'Art Egyptiens";
Leeman, "Aegyptiche Monumente";
Rossellini, "Monumenti Egitto";
Hottenroth, "Le Costume";
Racinet, "Le Costume Historique";
Sir J. G. Wilkinson, "Ancient Egyptians";

British Museum Handbooks and Reproductions.

These reproductions have lately been augmented and for those who cannot visit the Museum will be found most useful.

Plate I.

Plate I., which dates 700 B.C., is an exact copy of an Egyptian drawing. It will be noticed that the Egyptian method of representing the figure is a peculiar one. A modern representation of the same type of dress is shown in Fig. 2, and the plan of cutting in Fig. 2A. It should be noted that this plan—namely, a tunic with braces—is in some instances shown with the braces buttoned on each shoulder at the narrowest part. This illustration is given as a type of Egyptian dress decoration, which would be either printed, painted, or embroidered on the garment. It might be considered that this type of dress more nearly approaches the skirt than the tunic; but reaching, as it does, to the breast-line, and comparing various examples which, as it were, gradually merge into the sleeveless tunic which again merges into the tunic with short sleeves, the present classification will be found to be the most convenient.

M.G.H. del. *F.S H. pinx.*

A GODDESS

Plate II.

Plate II., which dates 1700 B.C. also first century B.C., is an exact copy of an Egyptian drawing of a woman wearing a species of tunic with braces (plan, Fig. 1). The striped decoration upon this tunic is suggested by the lines of another type of Egyptian dress—namely, the drawn-up skirt. The origin of the decoration can be easily understood by a reference to the drapery on Plate IX. In the original of this drawing the figure is represented with a lofty head-dress in addition to the fillet of ribbon and the golden asp here shown, but for the sake of getting the figure on a scale large enough to show clear details the head-dress is omitted. The person represented is said to be Cleopatra dressed as a goddess.

Fig. 1

M.G.H. del. *F.S.H. pinx.*

A QUEEN

Figs. 2, 3, and 4, dating 1700, 1500, and 3700 B.C. respectively, are wearing dresses of the first great type of Egyptian costume—namely, the tunic type. They were made of fairly thick linen. Fig. 2 is put on by stepping into it and pulling it up. Figs. 3 and 4 are put on over the head; the measurements given will fit a slim figure without underclothing. The origin of Fig. 2 was most probably a piece of linen of the same length as this garment but wide enough to lap about half round the figure and have a piece tucked in at the top to keep it closed. This sort of tight drapery is quite commonly worn by negresses in Africa to-day. We also find it on some ancient Egyptian wooden statuettes, the drapery being of linen while the figure only is in wood.

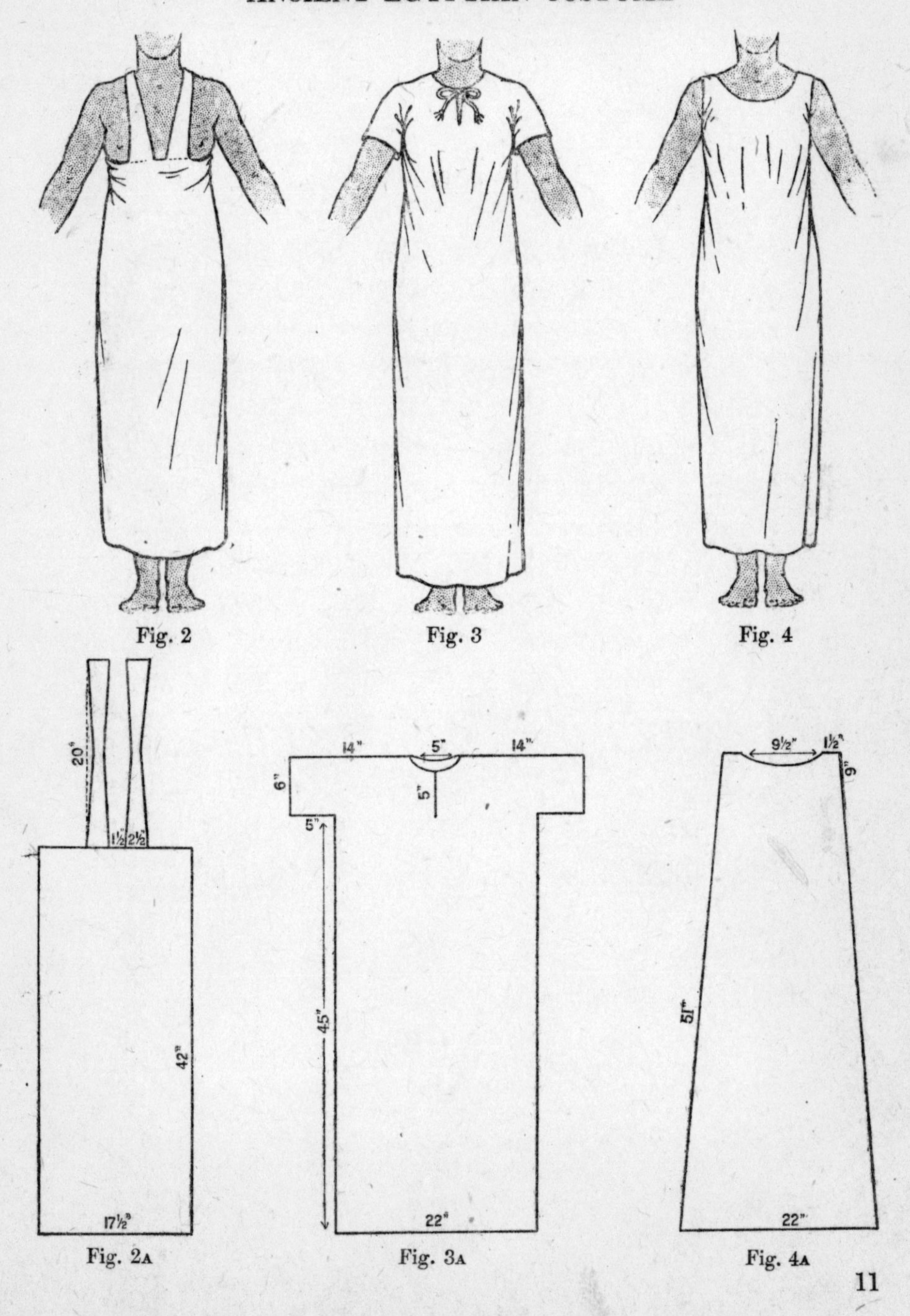

Fig. 2 Fig. 3 Fig. 4

Fig. 2A Fig. 3A Fig. 4A

Plate III.

It will be noticed that the Egyptian dress decoration is chiefly confined to the collar, which will be seen in wear on Plates V., VI., VIII., and X. The patterns were either embroidered, painted, beaded, or jewelled; the favourite lotus flower is almost always in evidence in the designs (see a, b, c, and d on Plate III.). On this plate also will be seen several other characteristic borders (f, g, h, i), and two all-over patterns (k, e), which were probably either stamped or tapestry-woven on the dress fabric. The colouring of these patterns is chiefly taken from *painted* representations of persons and ornaments. To arrive at the exact colouring used if the garments were decorated with dyed materials the description of the types of colours used in dyeing ancient Assyrian and Persian costumes, see p. 66, will give a more exact notion of what was worn. We have, in the British Museum, actual examples of dyed wools and coloured beads used in dress decoration.

PLATE III

F.S.H. fec.

DETAILS OF DECORATION

Plate IV.

Plate IV. belongs to the next great division of Egyptian costume, which may be called the "Type of the Robe." This illustration shows it in its simplest form—namely, ungirded. To understand the quaint Egyptian drawing of Plate IV. a reference to Fig. 5 is necessary, which is a modern drawing of the same costume. As will be seen from the plan, Fig. 5A, this garment consists of a piece of material twice the height of the figure and folded over in the middle; a hole is here cut for the neck and, in addition, a short slit down the front to allow of the garment being pulled over the head. The material is sewn up the sides from the bottom, leaving a space at the top for the passage of the arms. A garment similar in type to this is worn at the present day in Egypt and Syria, and also, strange to say, by the natives of Brazil.

This robe should be compared with that worn by Darius, King of Persia, later in this volume.

Fig. 5

Musicians are often represented wearing this robe, sometimes rounded off at each side of the hem so that it does not trail as it does on Fig. 5.

Fig. 5A

PLATE IV

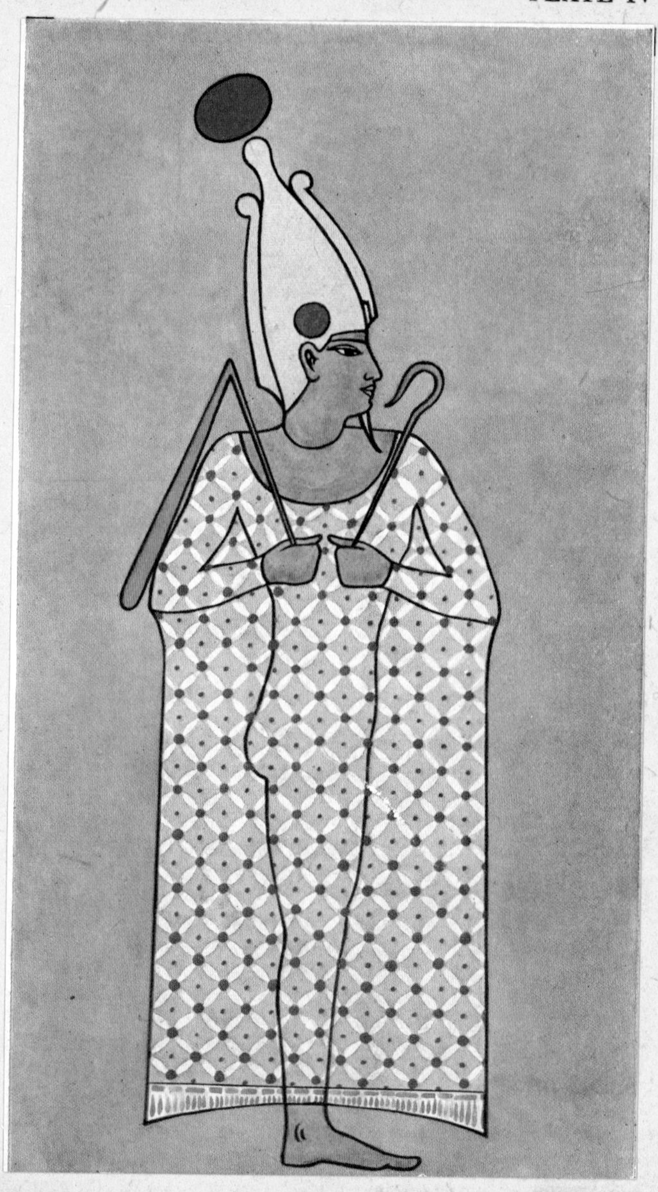

M.G.H. del. *F.S.H. pinx.*

THE GOD OSIRIS

Plate V.

Plate V., dating 1450 B.C., shows the same robe as Plate IV. worn in a different manner. In this case the garment is left open down the sides, the front half is taken and pinned at the back of the waist, and the back half is drawn towards the front and girded with a wide sash measuring 32″ × 120″, as shown in Plate V. and Figs. 6, 7, 8, and 9. It should be noted that Fig. 6 is a modern drawing of Plate V.; also the costume upon p. 19, which dates 2500 B.C., gives three different views of the same dress, a costume which emphasizes the love of the Egyptians for drawing up the dress tightly so as to define the limbs at the back and allowing great masses of drapery to fall in front to the feet. To adjust the sash or girdle on Plate V., commence at the right side of waist drawing the sash downwards to the left and round the hips at back, next draw upwards across the front from right to left and round waist at back and tuck the remaining length of sash in front as shown in Fig. 6.

M.G.H. del. *F.S.H. pinx.*

ANI, A SCRIBE

Fig. 6

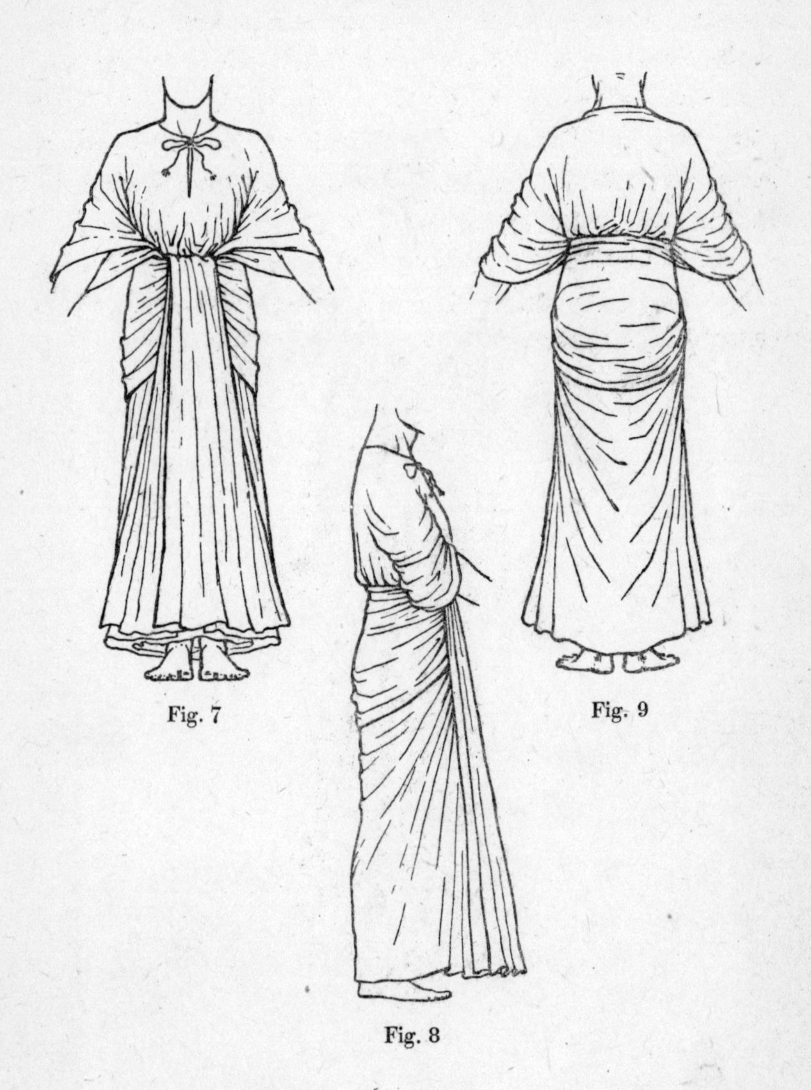

Fig. 7

Fig. 9

Fig. 8

Plate VI. is an illustration of a robe worn by a woman 1450 B.C., and Fig. 10 is a modern representation of the same robe. It will be noted in this case that the front half is not pinned behind the back, but is kept quite full in front, and that the back half, instead of being girded by a sash, is drawn round and tied in a knot just under the breast.

This robe on women is also sometimes tied with a narrow girdle under the breast instead of the edges being knotted.

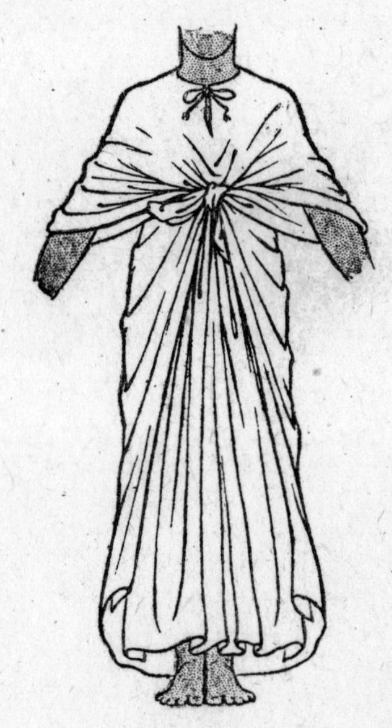

Fig. 10

PLATE VI

M.G.H. del. *F.S.H. pinx.*

THUTHU, WIFE OF ANI

Plate VII.

The decoration on this plate shows the detail of the characteristic Egyptian winged globe (a), hawk (b), and beetle (scarabæus) (c). Plates I. and VIII. are examples of the application of winged decoration upon Egyptian costume.

Three other geometrical borders (d, e, and f) and two all-over patterns (g and h) are given; g shows an example of the well-known feather or scale pattern; h (which is similar to e, Plate III.) is a favourite geometric motif, and was often printed or painted on garments. A very charming effect also of this pattern was a tunic entirely composed of beads, or beads and reeds, and worn over the garment shown on Fig. 2, p. 11. Several beaded networks of this type may be seen on the mummies in the British Museum.

DETAILS OF DECORATION

Plate VIII.

The third outstanding type of Egyptian costume may be described as the "Type of the Petticoat and Cape" (the petticoat was sometimes worn without the cape). Now this petticoat or skirt, as shown in Plate VIII. and Fig. 11, consists of a straight cut piece of material threaded through at the waist with a narrow strip which is knotted round the figure to keep the garment in position; the cape-like shoulder drapery is an oblong piece of stuff, to drape which take the corners d and e of Fig. 11A in your hands and twist them till the triangles a, b, c, and d, e, f, have become cords, and then knot as shown in the diagram. In the skirt piece, Fig. 11B, sew together the two short sides. As will be seen in the illustration, a long knotted girdle about 100 inches in length is worn over the skirt. It passes twice round the waist, and is knotted at the back as well as the front. In Plate VIII. the deep ornamental collar is worn over the cape. The collar, which was fastened down the back, is shown in plan (Fig. 11C).

Fig. 12 shows another method of wearing a similarly cut but rather longer skirt; in this case there is no waist cord; two pieces of the upper edge about half a yard apart are taken in the hands and twisted, one is crossed over the other and tucked inside, the other is pulled up and

M.G.H. del. *F.S.H. pinx.*

A QUEEN

forms an ear, as shown in sketch. This particular draping is the inspiration of the decoration on Plate II. Similar drapings without the twisting were worn both by men and women. It is interesting to note that a practically similar garment is worn in Burma at the present day by both men and women.

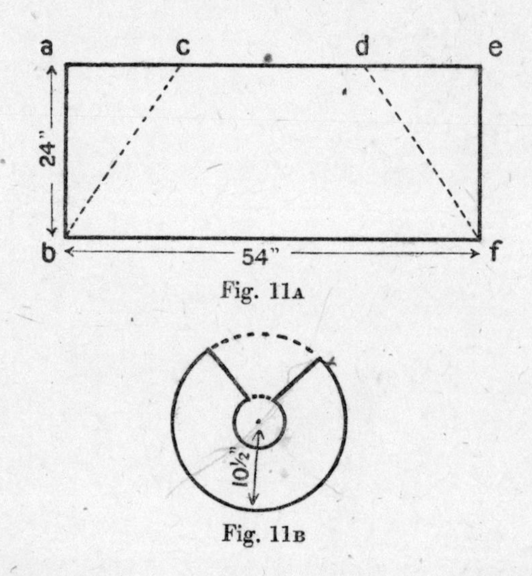

Fig. 11A

Fig. 11B

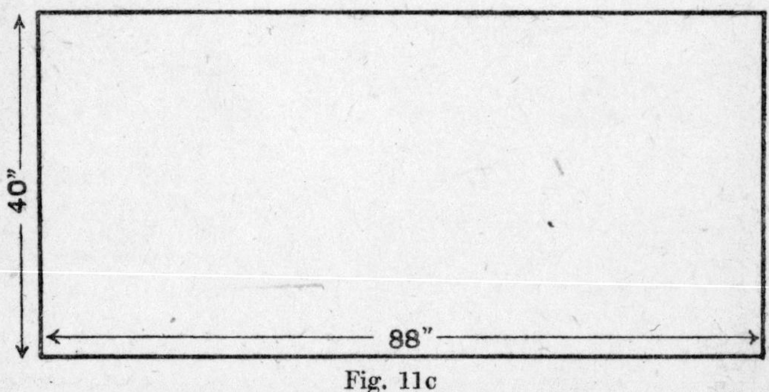

Fig. 11C

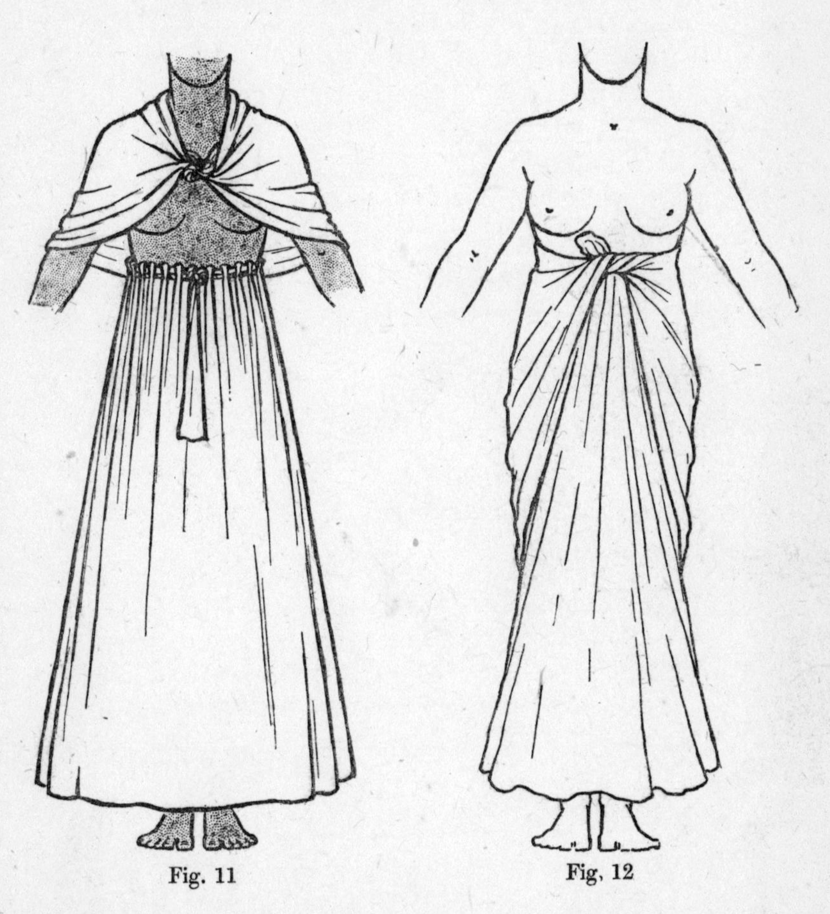

Fig. 11

Fig. 12

Compare Fig. 12 with Plate II. where the drapery here given has suggested in its lines a decoration of stripes.

Plate IX.

The noteworthy details of the decorations on this plate are those illustrated at a and b. These are appendages from girdles such as worn by male figures; an example is Fig. 21. The material of this appendage may be possibly of painted leather, wool embroidered linen, or linen with metal mounts. Many beautiful painted illustrations of this girdle appendage are to be found in the British Museum; e is from a feather fan.

F.S.H. *fec.*

DETAILS OF DECORATION

Fig. 13 is an Egyptian woman's costume dating 1450 B.C.; she is wearing two garments—namely, a skirt and cloak. This skirt, which is frequently worn alone without the cloak, as shown in Fig. 12, is cut to exactly the same width top and bottom. It is wide for the figure, and the superfluous fullness is caught up in each hand in the act of putting on. The upper edge of garment is drawn tightly round the figure just under the breasts; the portions held in each hand are then tied together in a knot. In Fig. 13 the cloak is knotted in with the skirt; this cloak is simply a rectangular piece of material. It will be noted that Figs. 13, 14, and 15 all show the popular Egyptian effect of drapery drawn tightly round the back of the limbs and falling full in front.

Fig. 14, which dates A.D. 200, shows a Roman adaptation of the same costume. The figure wears underneath a long tunic, and over this, tightening it in at the waist, an Egyptian skirt; a small Egyptian scarf is knotted to the skirt in similar fashion to the costume in Fig. 15. All the garments worn by Fig. 14 are rectangular pieces of material; the tunic is two straight pieces of stuff sewn up the sides; the top edge is divided into three parts by pinning; these openings form the neck and arm-holes.

Fig. 15 is a Greek costume of the fourth century B.C. in which the Egyptian influence is equally strongly marked; in this case, again, the garments are all rectangular pieces of material, the sleeves in one with the tunic. To knot the cloak to the over-skirt, as shown in this figure, the fullness of the over-skirt should be bunched up in one hand; the two corners of the cloak are taken in the other hand and twisted together round the skirt in a knot.

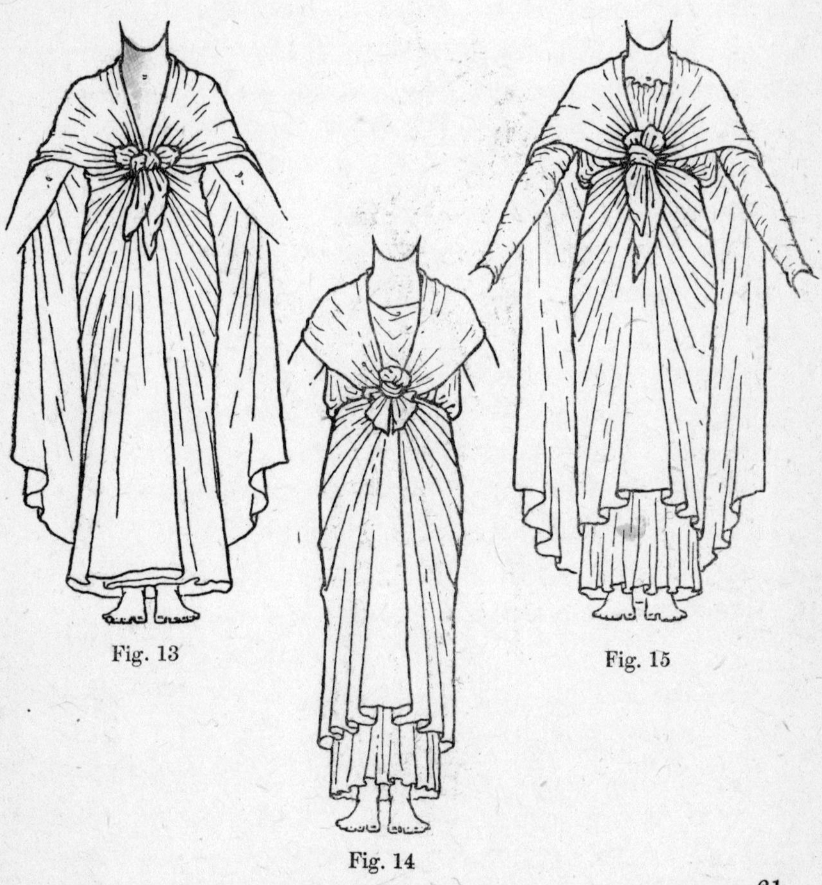

Fig. 13

Fig. 14

Fig. 15

Plate X.

Plate X. shows the fourth division of Egyptian costume — namely, the "Type of the Shawl or Drapery." Several varieties of this type are illustrated and described on pp. 33, 34, and 35.

Fig. 16

A PRIESTESS

The fourth division of Egyptian costume is shown in the examples on Plate X. and pp. 33, 34, and 35. These are the draped or shawl type of costume. They have many resemblances to the draping of the well-known Indian sari of modern times. Compare these with illustration of sari (p. 39). The ingenuity displayed in the draping of these costumes can only be realized when they are actually done upon a model. It should be noted with regard to all Egyptian costumes of the more fully draped type that the entire draperies

Figs. 16A and 17A

seem to radiate from one point, usually a knot at the waist, with very beautiful effect.

To drape Fig. 16, which is a modern drawing of Plate X., tie a cord round the waist, tuck in corner b (see plan, Fig. 16A) at left side of waist, pass round the back and round the right side to front again; make some pleats and tuck them in in centre front of waist, then pass round back again to right side; catch up the whole drapery and throw it upwards from right-hand side of waist under left arm-pit, pass on round the back

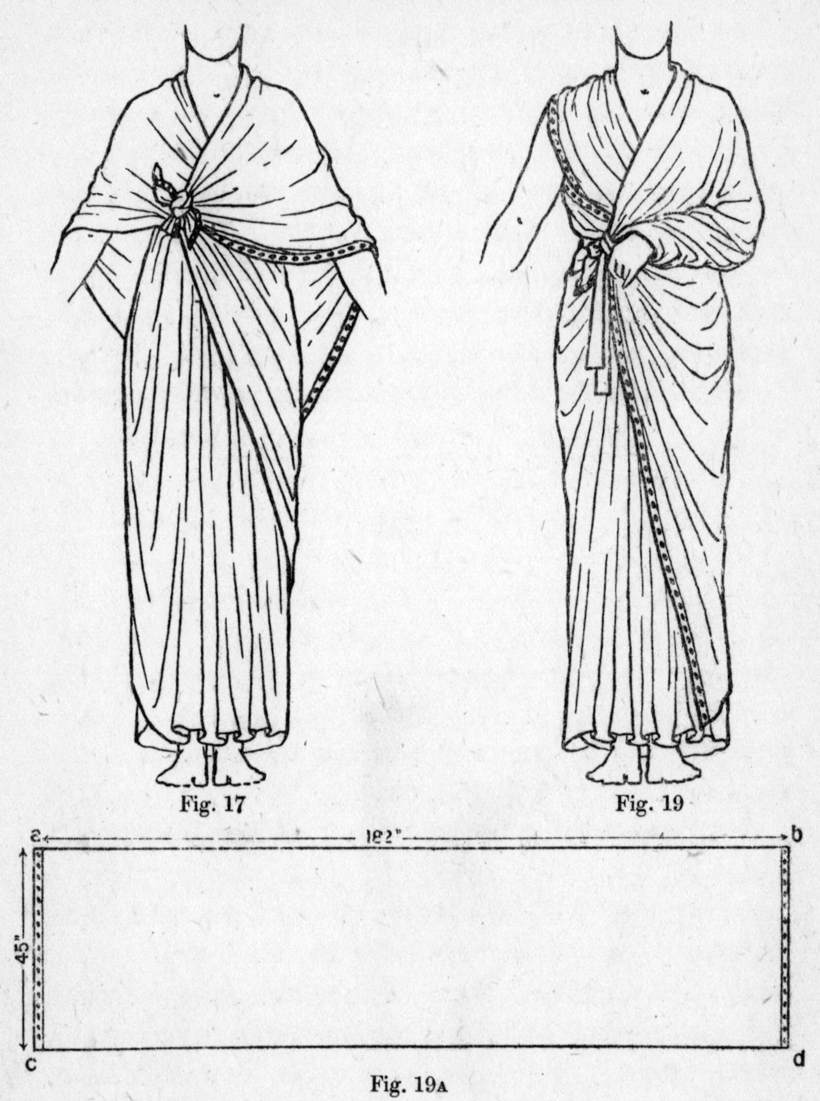

Fig. 17

Fig. 19

Fig. 19A

The width 45″ will drape a tall figure, say 5′ 6″ in height. The drapery should be narrower for a lesser height.

and over the right shoulder towards front, then throw the remaining portion of garment across the chest and backwards over the left shoulder; take corner a and bring it round under right arm-pit, release corner b which you first tucked in, and tie it to corner a. The corner c will hang down in a point at the back.

To drape the costume on Fig. 17, which dates 1300 B.C., take the corner a of Fig. 17A and hold it at right side of waist in front, pass round the back and round the left side to front again, tuck in some pleats in centre front, and pass on round the back to left side of waist under left arm towards the front; catch up the entire garment and throw over the right shoulder, pass the upper edge of the garment round the back of the neck and over the left shoulder and downwards across the breast to right, where the corner b should be tied to corner a. Corner d hangs down in a point at the back.

For Fig. 18, which dates 1600 B.C., take the corner a of Fig. 18A and hold it at right side of waist in front, pass the edge a-b round back of waist to the left side and across the front of waist, pass it round the right side again under the right arm towards the back and upwards over the left shoulder; tie the corner a to corner b in front.

For Fig. 19, which dates 550 B.C., tie a waist cord, hold corner a of Fig. 19A at left side of waist in front, and throw the whole garment upwards over the right shoulder to the back; take the corner c, bring it round under the right arm, and hold it along with the corner a; draw the edge a-b, which still hangs over the right shoulder, downwards across the back to left side of waist. Bring it round

Fig. 18

Fig. 18A

to front of waist and pin it to the corners a and c at the left side of waist in front, passing the garment on round the front; tuck in a few pleats in centre front into the waist cord, then pass it round right side of waist and upwards across the back over the left shoulder, downwards across the breast to right side of waist; here pass a loop of material over the left wrist as shown in diagram; now pass a girdle round the waist over the entire drapery, knot it at right side of waist, confining the drapery as illustrated in Fig. 19.

Here are three other varieties of Egyptian costume. Fig. 20, which dates sixth century B.C., is an arrangement of a cloak worn by a man (Plan 20A). Fig. 21 shows an interesting cross-over garment sheathing the upper part of the body, worn by a Warrior King, 1200 B.C. It was probably made of leather or quilted linen (plan, Fig. 21A). This figure is also wearing one of the characteristic belts with appendages (for detail see Plate IX., a and b). Fig. 22, which dates 1300 B.C., is wearing a robe, as previously described on Fig. 6, but in addition has a stiff corselet (Plan 22A) of leather or quilted linen which is fastened at the side; the date of this figure is 1300 B.C.

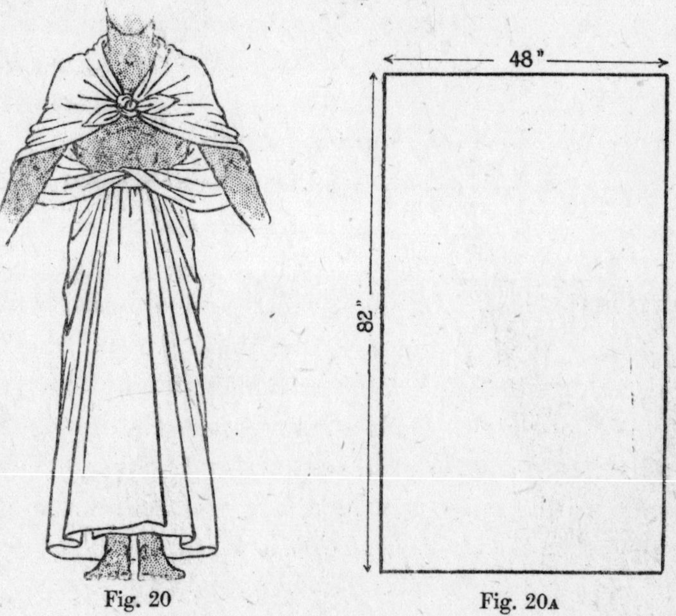

Fig. 20

Fig. 20A

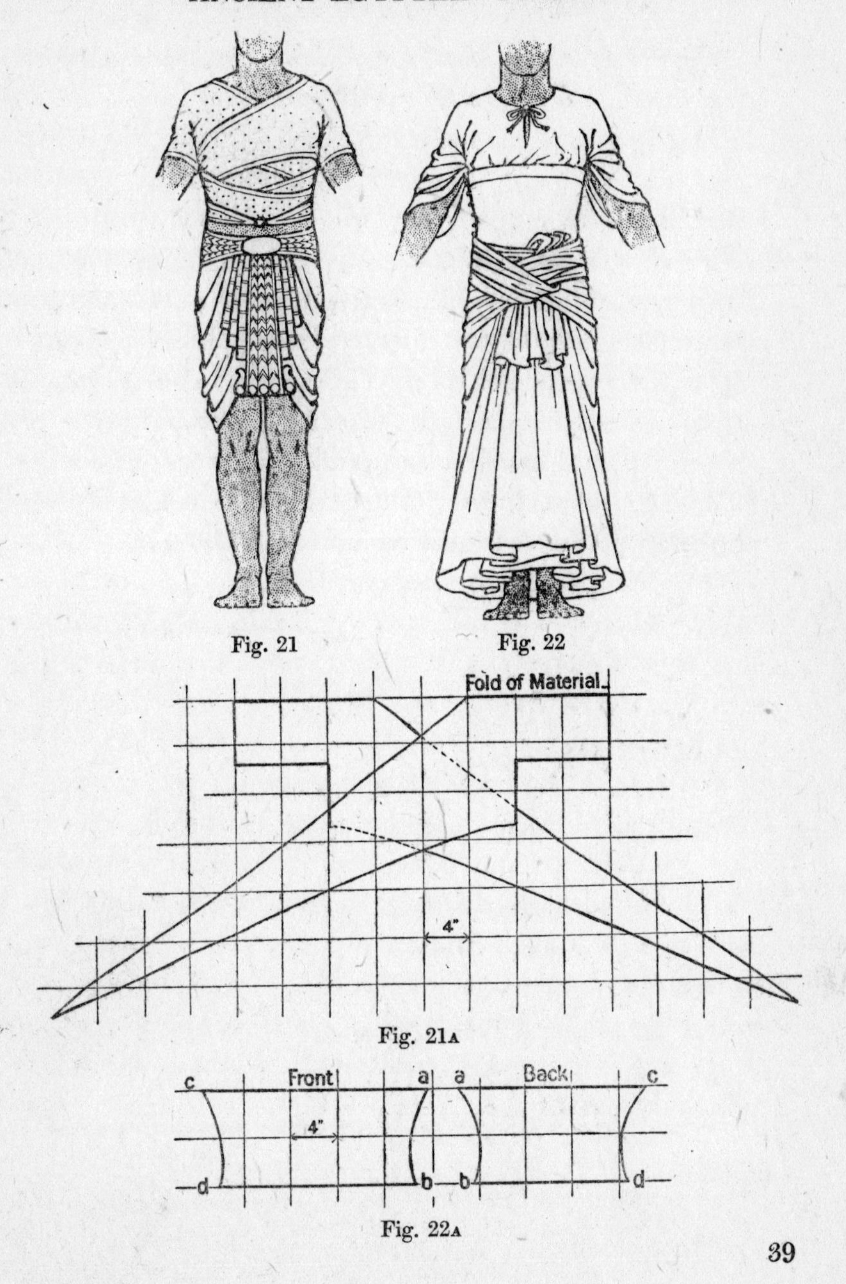

Fig. 21

Fig. 22

Fig. 21A

Fig. 22A

A COMPARISON

THE INDIAN "SARI"

Before passing from Egyptian costume, it seems interesting to compare the accompanying illustrations of an ordinary present-day draping worn by women in India. This long shawl drapery (the "sari") presents extraordinary similarities to some of the ancient Egyptian shawls or draperies already illustrated.

The method of draping is as follows: Tie a waist cord; take the corner b and fix it to the right-hand side of waist, then pass the edge b-a across the front of waist, round the left side towards the back, and round the back of waist again to the right side; now take up some pleats in the drapery and push them inside the waist cord in centre front of waist, then pass on the drapery round the waist to back and round to the right sdie again. Now catch up all the remaining drapery and throw it upwards across the chest over the left shoulder. Let the corner c hang down the back, and bring the corner a round towards the front of waist and tuck it in at the left side of waist, so that it will have the thrown-over portion to the right of it. This completes this draping of an Indian sari. The width of this sari will drape a figure of 5′ 4″, most of those worn by Indian women are narrower.

A COMPARISON: THE INDIAN SARI

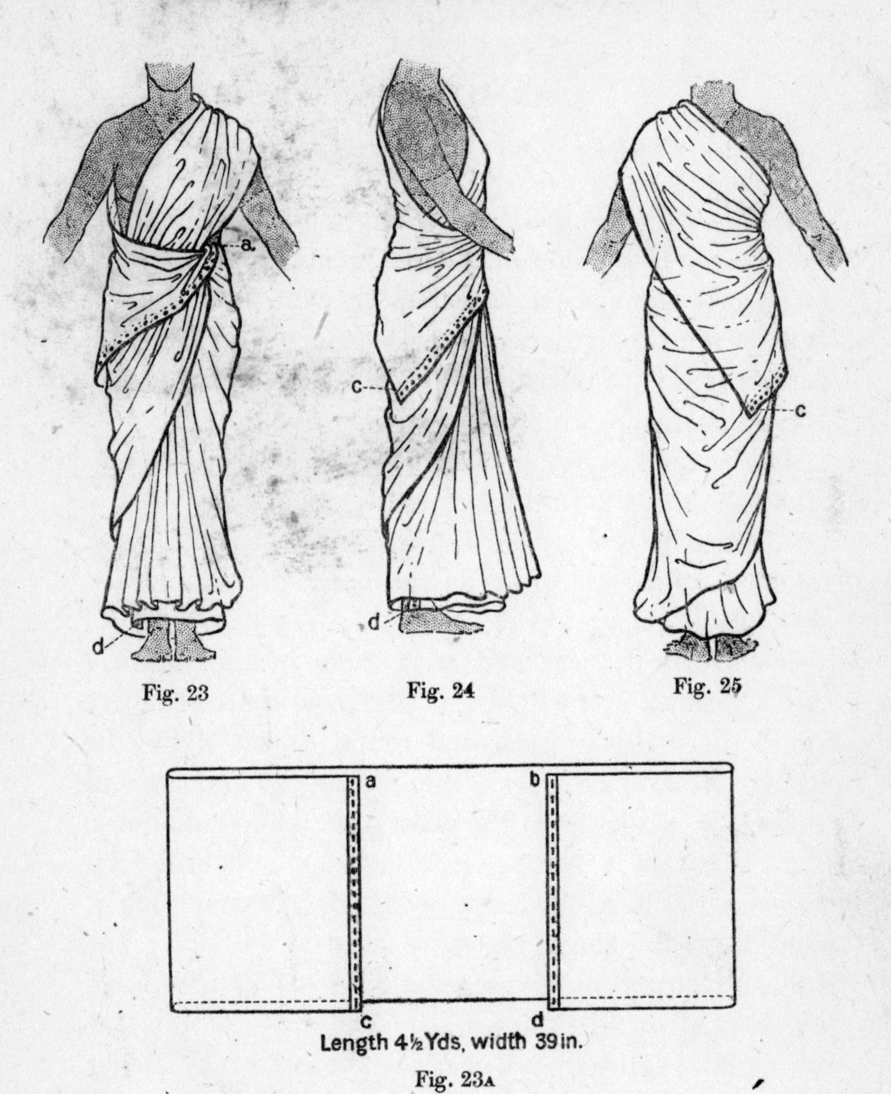

Fig. 23

Fig. 24

Fig. 25

Fig. 23A

ANCIENT ASSYRIAN COSTUME

GENERAL DESCRIPTION
OF
ANCIENT ASSYRIAN COSTUME

CUTTING OUT

THERE are practically only two types of garment generally found in the representations of ancient Assyrian costume: (1) the *shawl*, and (2) the *tunic*. These vary in size and proportion, and are worn either alone, but more generally in combination.

DECORATION

Except in the earliest examples, decoration is lavish in Assyrian costume; in fact, the costume of a King when at its richest may be said to be absolutely covered with ornament. Jewellery, woven and embroidered patterns, and fringes are used in the utmost profusion. See the illustrations of the most characteristic ornamental details of this style.

MATERIAL

The materials used seem to have been of linen and wool. The skins and furs of animals and metal were also in use, but chiefly for military and hunting costume.

DATES

The earliest type of costume here shown is a rather elaborate shawl drapery worn without any tunic underneath. Later comes the tunic with various fringed shawl draperies worn in addition, and some of the latest types have the tunic worn alone without the shawl draperies. The dates given for the costumes illustrated in this style have been verified at the British Museum. It should be remembered, as in the case of ancient Egyptian costume, that the dresses changed very slowly indeed, and most styles of this era were worn literally for hundreds of years.

MEN AND WOMEN: THE DIFFERENCE IN THEIR DRESS

The representations of costume which Assyrian art has left us are almost entirely those of men's dress. Two examples of women's dresses are shown in this volume. The first wears a plain ungirded tunic and a simply draped shawl covering the figure partially. The second is the dress of a Queen, and has the tunic almost entirely covered with a voluminous shawl. The wide belt with narrow belt over it seems to be confined to the men's costume, as also the tighter and scantier shawl draperies which exist in singular variety.

For Assyrian and Ancient Persian Styles consult: Layard's "Monuments of Nineveh"; Flandin and Coste, "Voyage en Perse"; Botta, "Monuments de Ninïve"; Victor Place, "Ninïve et Assyrie"; Perrot and Chipiez, "History of Art in Persia"; Racinet, "Le Costume Historique"; Hottenroth "Le Costume." Also reproductions and handbooks of the collections in the British Museum.

Figs. 26, 27, and 28: This drapery is from the figure of the King Gudea, 2500 B.C. (see British Museum). To drape, place the corner b of Fig. 26A under left arm-pit, and draw the edge b-a round the back of shoulders under the right arm-pit, across the front of chest, and round the back again, and under the right arm-pit once more; then throw the edge b-a upwards across the chest and over the left shoulder; the corner a will then hang down the back. Take this corner a and tuck it in at the right side of breast, as shown in illustration (Fig. 26). It should be noted that, unless the left hand is raised, the left arm and hand are entirely covered by this drapery, the right arm only being left free for movement. This dignified drapery presents points of similarity to the Roman "toga" of a much later period.

ANCIENT ASSYRIAN COSTUME

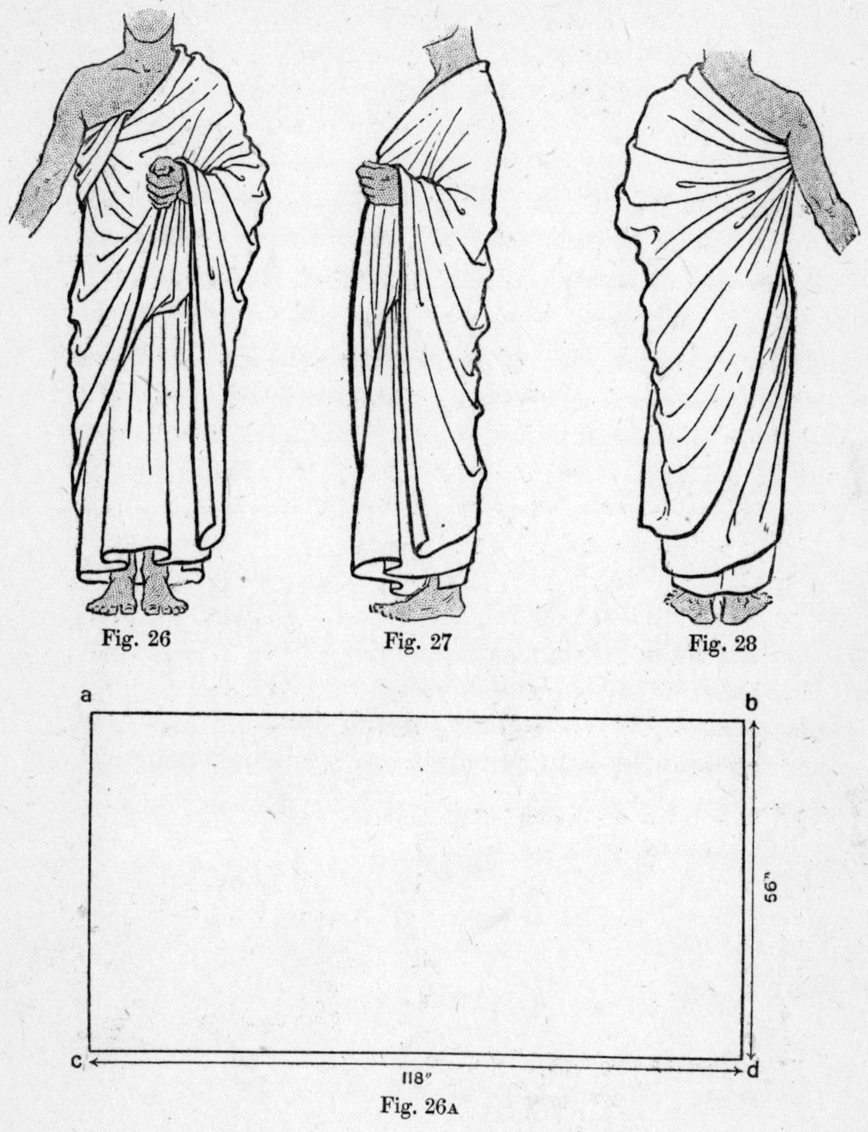

Fig. 26 Fig. 27 Fig. 28

Fig. 26A

Plate XI.—This type of dress, which in the British Museum is described as worn by "a Mythological Figure in attendance upon King Assur-nasir-pal," ninth century B.C., might be dated about 1000 B.C., as following the usual custom of the ancients who dressed their sacred figures in the costume of some previous generation as a rule, consists of a simple tunic with short sleeves, and reaching to the knee, cut in similar fashion to the Egyptian; then a small shawl (Fig. 29B) is wrapped round the hips, beginning with the corner a on right hip, and passing the edge a-b across the front towards the left and round the waist. The triangle b-e-f can be tucked in at waist-line; then the wide belt, probably leather, which is coloured buff in the illustration, is put on and kept in position by the narrow belt, which is coloured red; this belt is much better seen in Fig. 30. Lastly, the large shawl (Fig. 29A) has the corner b tucked in to narrow belt at left side of waist, and the edge a-b passed round the back towards the right side of waist upwards across the chest, and hangs down the back over the left shoulder. The original of this figure is winged, the wings being omitted here.

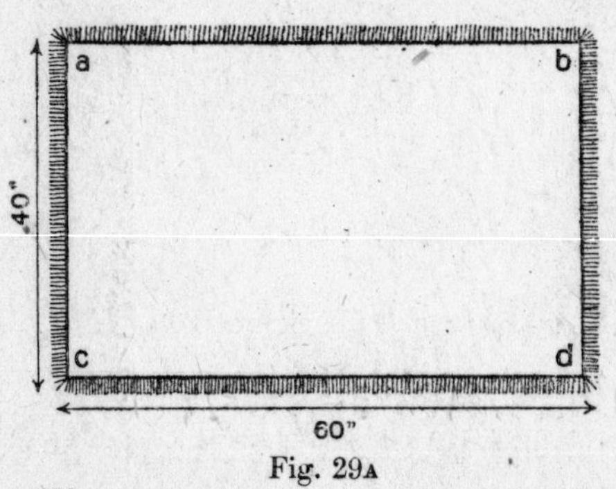

Fig. 29A

Fig. 29B

M.G.H. del. *F.S.H. pinx.*

MYTHOLOGICAL PERSONAGE

Fig. 30 represents King Assur-nasir-pal (ninth century B.C.) wearing a tunic of similar type to Plate XI., but long. Tied at his waist and covering the back half of his figure is a small richly decorated shawl about 20 inches square. Note the tassels hanging from right-hand bottom corner; these would be the same on the left-hand bottom corner. He also wears the belt mentioned in connection with Plate XI. The wavy tassels which look like horsehair hang from his sword belt; a tassel also hangs from the back of his necklace, and two ribbons from his cap-band. Note the similarity of this cap to the so-called fez or tarbush worn in Assyria at the present day.

Fig. 30

Fig. 31: The point to be noted in this figure is the arrangement of a fringe drapery which goes once round the waist, is thrown over one shoulder, and hangs down the back.

Fig. 31

Fig. 32: This man, in hunting dress, ninth century B.C., has a small scarf, fringed only at the ends, wrapped tightly round the limbs, reaching to the knee.

Fig. 32

Fig. 33: This woman, a captive of Sennacherib who reigned in eighth and seventh centuries B.C., wears a long tunic, and over it a long shawl fringed at the two ends and measuring 50″ × 80″. To drape this shawl, place one corner under the left arm-pit and draw it across the back under the right arm-pit, wrapping it once round the body; draw it across the back and up over right shoulder. A corner of the fringed end will hang down in front of the right shoulder.

Fig. 33

PLATE XII.

Plate XII. shows a number of characteristic Assyrian ornaments.

a, The sacred tree.

b, c, d, e, f, Repeating patterns on costumes.

g, h, i, j, k, l, Borders on costumes.

m, One of the many rosettes much used in Assyrian decorations.

These should be compared with the decorated costumes shown in the plates; they would be either woven or embroidered.

F.S.H. fec.

DETAILS OF DECORATION

PLATE XIII.—A facsimile drawing, from an enamel tile, is one of the many representations of the King Assur-nasir-pal, ninth century B.C. The description of his dress will be better understood by referring to Figs. 34, 35, and 36. The King wears over his long tunic a very beautiful and dignified shawl drapery, which

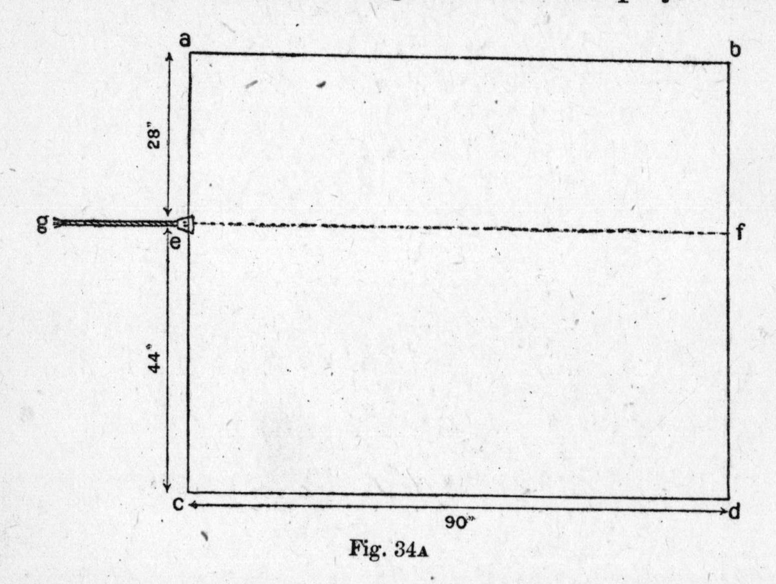

Fig. 34A

is fringed, recalling certain Egyptian types already illustrated, and, indeed, has points of similarity with certain Greek and Roman draperies. To drape this shawl (see Fig. 34A) fold over on the line e-f so that e-f, a-b, hangs down outside; then attach the cord e-g as illustrated, and hold g at right side of waist in front, throwing the rest of the shawl backwards over the right shoulder. Draw the edge e-f round the back of neck, and form a

M.G.H. del. *F.S.H. pinx.*

KING ASSUR-NASIR-PAL

sling over the left arm, as shown. To complete the draping, continue to pass the edge e-f round the waist towards the right, passing under the right elbow, then on round the back and left side until it reaches about 6 inches in front of left side of waist; now fold the remainder of drapery underneath, as shown in the drawings, and tie a cord round waist to keep all firmly in position; knot the end of the cord e-g to this waist cord. Fig. 35 shows the back view, and Fig. 36 shows the drapery thrown off the left shoulder to give freedom to both arms, Figs. 34 and 35 only giving freedom to the right arm. If the cord e-g is pulled down so that e touches the waist, then both shoulders will be covered by the drapery. Fig. 34 is the most usual arrangement of this type of drapery, but in looking at Plate XIII. closely it will be seen that the modern drawing (Fig. 37) is a more exact rendering. This drawing is from a draping of the same shawl as Fig. 34 is wearing, but the fold-over is somewhat deeper, the point e is tied closely to waist belt, and the drapery is rolled at waist while it is being adjusted. When worn thus, with a roll, the drapery will remain in position without the waist cord being tied over it, but it is more secure when it has been thus confined. Fig. 38 is still another variety of this type of draping, and is taken from a small statue of Assur-nasir-pal in the British Museum; there we have two shawls, one square and one semicircular (see Figs. 38A and 38B). To arrange this drapery, take the square shawl and fold outwards about 20 inches, as at e-f. Tie a waist cord on the tunic, and tuck the corner

Fig. 34

Fig. 36

Fig. 35

F

f deeply into it at left side of waist cord; then draw tightly round the figure in front and round again across the back of waist till the left side is reached again. Now double about 6 inches of the shawl inwards, and tuck again into waist cord. Take the semicircular shawl g-h, and attach the cord to another waist cord, throw backwards over the right shoulder, and arrange a sling over the left arm as before in Figs. 34 and 37. The corner h of the shawl shows in front about 8 inches below the waist towards the left. Tie the second waist cord tightly over this shawl to keep in position.

NOTE ON THE COLOURING OF ANCIENT ASSYRIAN AND PERSIAN COSTUMES

Though we do not possess the actual specimens of these costumes, still we can infer from the lavish ornament, and, from references in the Hebrew Old Testament writings, that rich colouring prevailed. The dyes were probably similar to those of ancient Egypt, and this table will suggest the particular hue of each colour:

Ancient Egyptian and Assyrian Dye Colours

Blue: Usually rather a dark indigo, sometimes paler.
Red: Much like the colour known as Indian red.
Yellow: Similar to yellow ochre.
Green: Much like the paint known as green bice, but rather more dull.
Purple: Dark, and quite a brownish hue of purple.

All these colours could be used as embroideries on a white or natural coloured ground of linen, the embroideries being of wool. In other cases the whole garment might be coloured throughout.

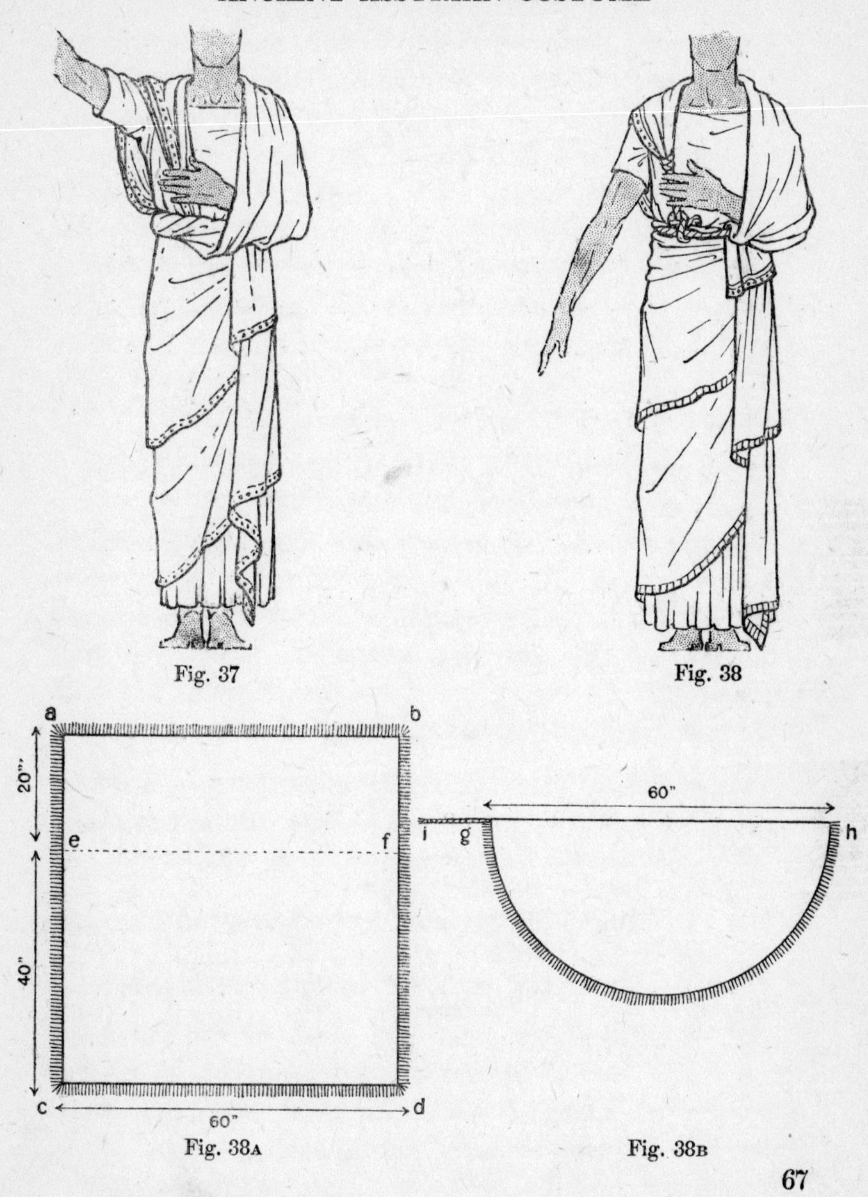

Fig. 37

Fig. 38

Fig. 38A

Fig. 38B

Fig. 39 is the tunic of King Assur-bani-pal, seventh century B.C. It will be noticed that it is cut very much in the same manner as the Egyptian tunic; the neck opening, which is a slit large enough to admit the head, does not show in the drawing, but three buttons on either side of neck will be seen. A row of fringe decorates the bottom, and the whole is richly embroidered; over this tunic were worn the wide and narrow belts.

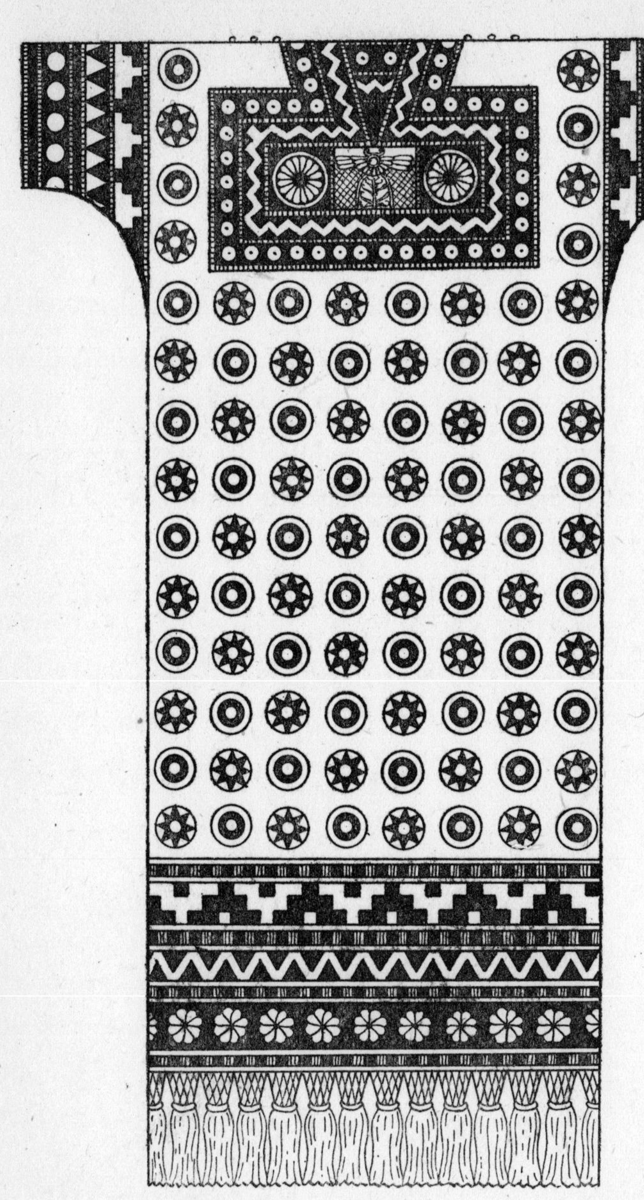

Fig. 39

Plate XIV.

Plate XIV. is the Queen of Assur-bani-pal, seventh century B.C. She wears a similar tunic to the King, but the sleeves reach half-way down the lower arm; her shawl, which is fringed all round, would measure 50″ × 130″. It is wrapped once round the lower limbs, and so covers the bottom of her tunic; it is then wound round the upper part of her body in similar fashion to that of the woman on p. 59, save that it goes in the opposite direction.

PLATE XIV

M.G.H. del. *F.S.H pinx.*

QUEEN OF ASSUR-BANI-PAL

PLATE XV.

Plate XV. shows further details of Assyrian decoration; attention may be particularly drawn to the varied forms of the tassels.

a, b, c, Bracelets.

d, e, f, Ear-rings.

g, h, i, j, Tassels from costumes and harness on horses.

k, Winged globe.

l, Palm tree.

m, Lappet of a King's tiara.

n, Bronze vessel.

o, Sword handle.

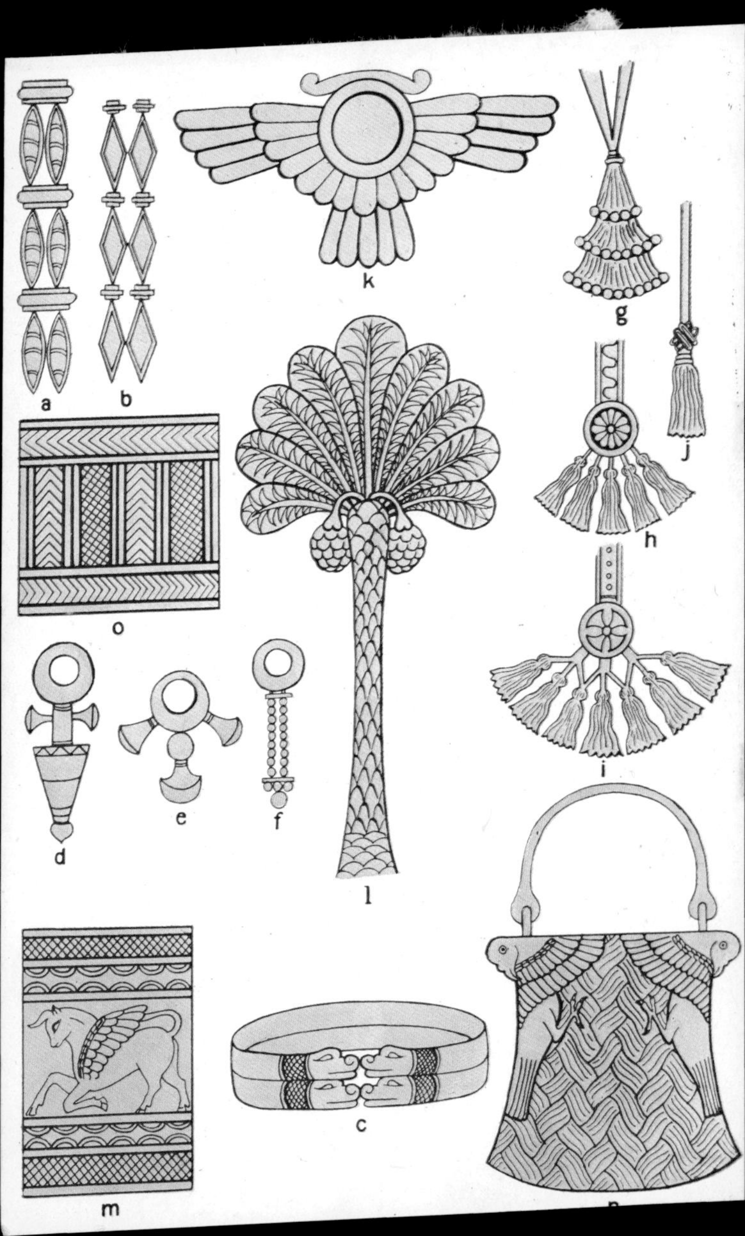

a
b
k
g
j
h
o
l
i
d
e
f
m
c

F.S.H. fec.

DETAILS OF DECORATION

ANCIENT PERSIAN COSTUME

GENERAL DESCRIPTION
OF
ANCIENT PERSIAN COSTUME

ALSO INCLUDING TWO EXAMPLES FROM CAPTIVE NATIONS

CUTTING OUT

THE garments illustrated in this style are of four types; of these, three have already appeared in the two previous styles—namely, the type of the *tunic,* the type of the *robe,* and the type of the *shawl* or drapery. In ancient Persian costume we come for the first time to type five: the *coat.* We may refer here also for the first time to the wearing of trousers, for these are usually shown worn with the coats in ancient Persian costume, and a diagram is given on p. 86 showing one of the earliest known methods of cutting these garments.

DECORATION

Ancient Persian decoration was so exceedingly similar to ancient Assyrian that it does not seem necessary to illustrate it. We do not find, however, that ancient Persian garments were ornamented to anything like the same extent as ancient Assyrian; the frequent fringes of the ancient Assyrian costumes were not nearly so lavishly employed in the ancient Persian style.

MATERIAL

Linen and wool were most probably the chief materials used in ancient Persian costume, but there are indications that leather may have been rather extensively employed in the more tight-fitting garments.

It must not be taken that either in Assyrian or ancient Persian dress the garments fitted as smoothly and tightly as might be imagined from the sculptured and painted representations; it is true folds are sometimes indicated, but the chief concern of the artists of both styles was to show the human figure and richly decorative ornament.

DATES

The illustrations here given of ancient Persian costumes date about the sixth and fifth centuries B.C. with two of neighbouring nations dating eighth century B.C. and sixth and fifth centnries B.C. respectively.

MEN AND WOMEN: THE DIFFERENCE IN THEIR DRESS

There is not sufficient information to form a definite picture of the women's dress of this period and style;

most probably it was a simple tunic and shawl like that worn in Assyria, but an interesting fact is that we have a representation of the Queen of a Persian King who reigned in the fifth century A.D. who is wearing trousers, which, it will be remembered, are worn by Persian women of the present day. In this connection it may be noted that the history of costume, as developed through the use of woven materials, presents a much more simple aspect than the history of those styles bearing evidences of having been first cut from leather. A moment's reflection will make it clear that in the case of woven stuffs the most economical system of cutting, and indeed the most obvious, for the primitive dress fashioner, was based on the rectangle. On the other hand, the fashioner of leather garments would naturally try to fit the human body with, as it were, a second skin, hence trousers and tight-fitting jackets may appear in very early civilizations.

For list of authorities see Ancient Assyrian Costume.

PLATE XVI. is a representation of Darius, King of Persia, sixth and fifth centuries B.C.; he is wearing the Median "Robe of Honour." It will be seen from the plan (Fig. 40A) that this robe is sewn up each side, leaving a space of 20 inches on either side for the hands. Like the Egyptian robe, the material required is twice the height of the figure, the material is doubled, a neck-hole cut, and the garment is pulled on over the head. The Persian or Median method of wearing the garment is unique: a girdle is tightly bound round the waist, and then the robe is pulled up at either side over the girdle so as to produce the very elegant effect shown in Plate XVI. and Fig. 40, which is a modern drawing of the front view of Plate XVI., the result giving great freedom to the arms. The King seems to have two robes of the same cut, one under the other.

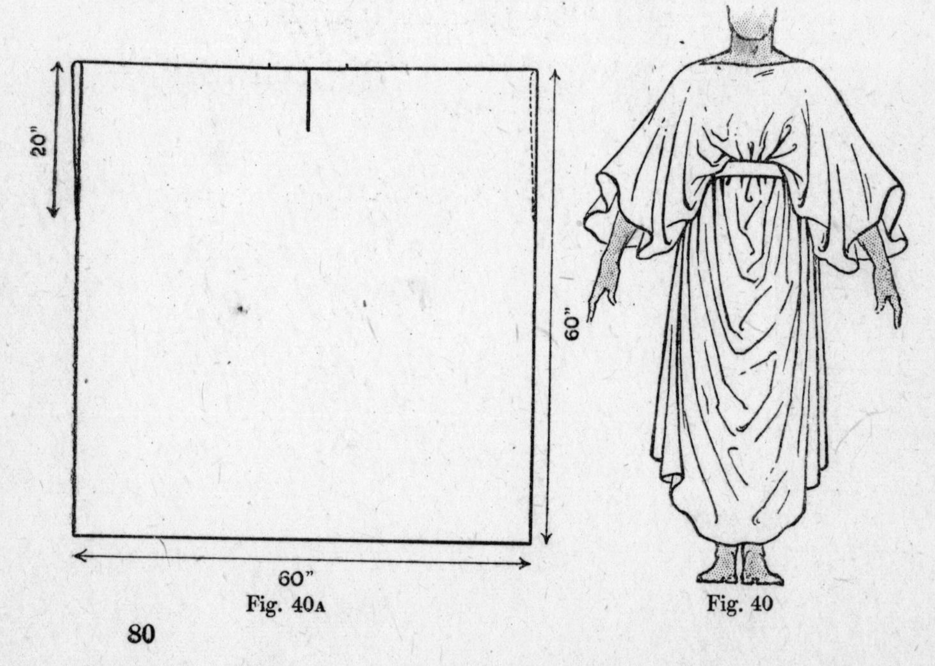

Fig. 40A

Fig. 40

M.G.H. del. *F.S.H. pinx.*

DARIUS, KING OF PERSIA

To arrange the drapery, dating sixth to fifth centuries B.C., on Fig. 41, take the corner b of Fig. 41A in the left hand, letting the rest of the drapery fall down the back, draw the edge b-a across the back, then under the right arm-pit across the chest, and throw the corner a upwards and over the left shoulder; a will hang down the back. It will be noted that this garment is weighted at the corners; this keeps it in position.

Fig. 42 is a modern drawing showing the garment in front view.

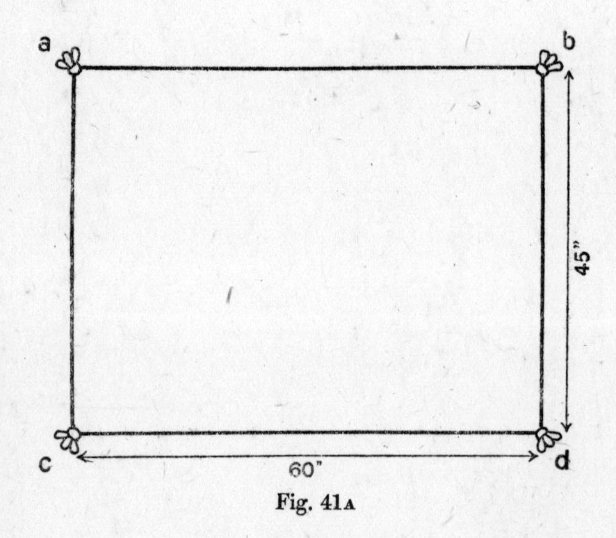

Fig. 41A

Fig. 42

Fig. 41

Fig. 43, dating eighth century B.C., is wearing cloak (see Fig. 43A) partly fringed. It is worn much in the same manner as Fig. 41, but in Fig. 43 the corner a is thrown backwards over the left shoulder, and the edge a-b is passed across the chest and under the right arm-pit, then drawn across the back, and the corner b falls down in front of the left shoulder.

This costume is not Persian, but that of some nation to the east of Persia in northern Asia Minor. The wearing of boots with upturned toes as here shown seems to have extended from Persia across northern Asia Minor to the Mediterranean even as far west as Italy.

Fig. 44 is a modern drawing showing the garment in front view.

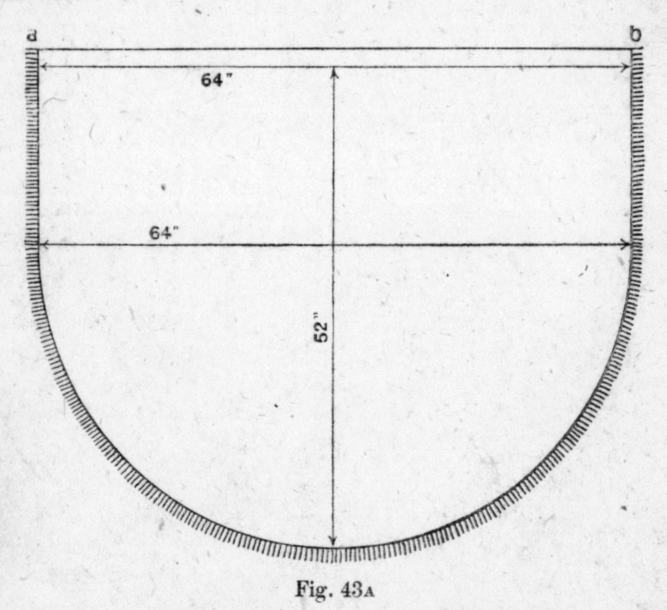

Fig. 43A

Fig. 44

Fig. 43

Fig. 45 is wearing a short-sleeved coat over a tunic. The edging shown is probably uncut fringe; in reality it would not fit the figure neatly, as the ancient artist has indicated, but would hang rather loosely.

Fig. 45A shows the method of cutting.

The costume is considered to be that of a Jewish captive of the Persian conqueror and dates sixth to fifth centuries B.C.

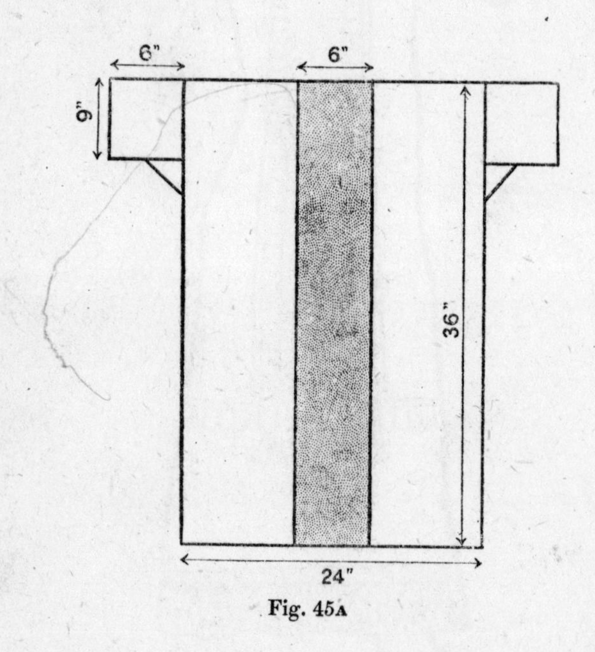

Fig. 45A

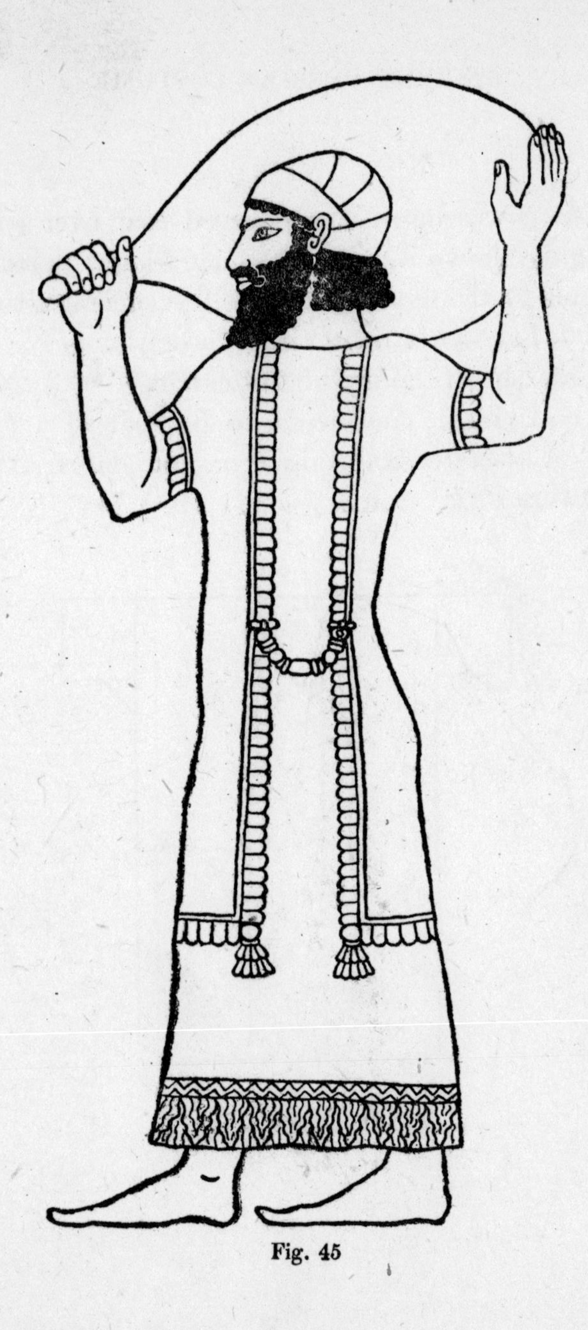

Fig. 45

Fig. 46, which dates sixth to fifth centuries B.C., is wearing over a tunic and trousers (see Fig. 46B) an overcoat with a set-in sleeve (see Fig. 46B), turned-over collar and cuffs, and tied in front with ribbons. The plan (Fig. 46A) shows one of the earliest known methods of setting in the sleeve; the collar in this plan is represented turned forward and lying flat.

The tunic worn by this figure, under his long overcoat, and also the trousers would most probably be of leather.

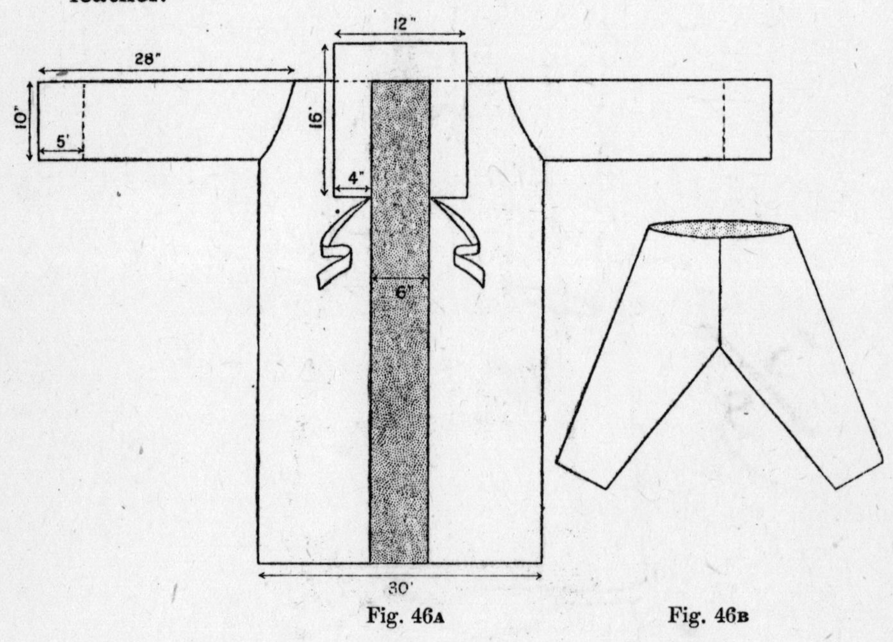

Fig. 46A

Fig. 46B

Fig. 46